INAUGURATION

A Celebration of Democracy

Find Our Children's Books at Amazon, IngramSpark, Lulu, Barnes & Noble, Target, and Other Retailers Worldwide. Find Publishing & Consulting Services, Our Book Podcast, YouTube Channel, Educational Blog, and so much more at: www.SlothDreamsBooks.com or www.PictureBookPro.org

**www.SlothDreamsBooks.com
www.PictureBookPro.org
www.ThePictureBookPro.org**

INAUGURATION DAY:
A Celebration of Democracy
Written & Illustrated
by KeriAnne Jelinek

What is Inauguration Day?

Inauguration Day is a special event in the United States when the President and Vice President officially begin their new terms in office.

This happens every four years on January 20th, marking the peaceful transfer of power—a tradition that shows the strength of democracy.

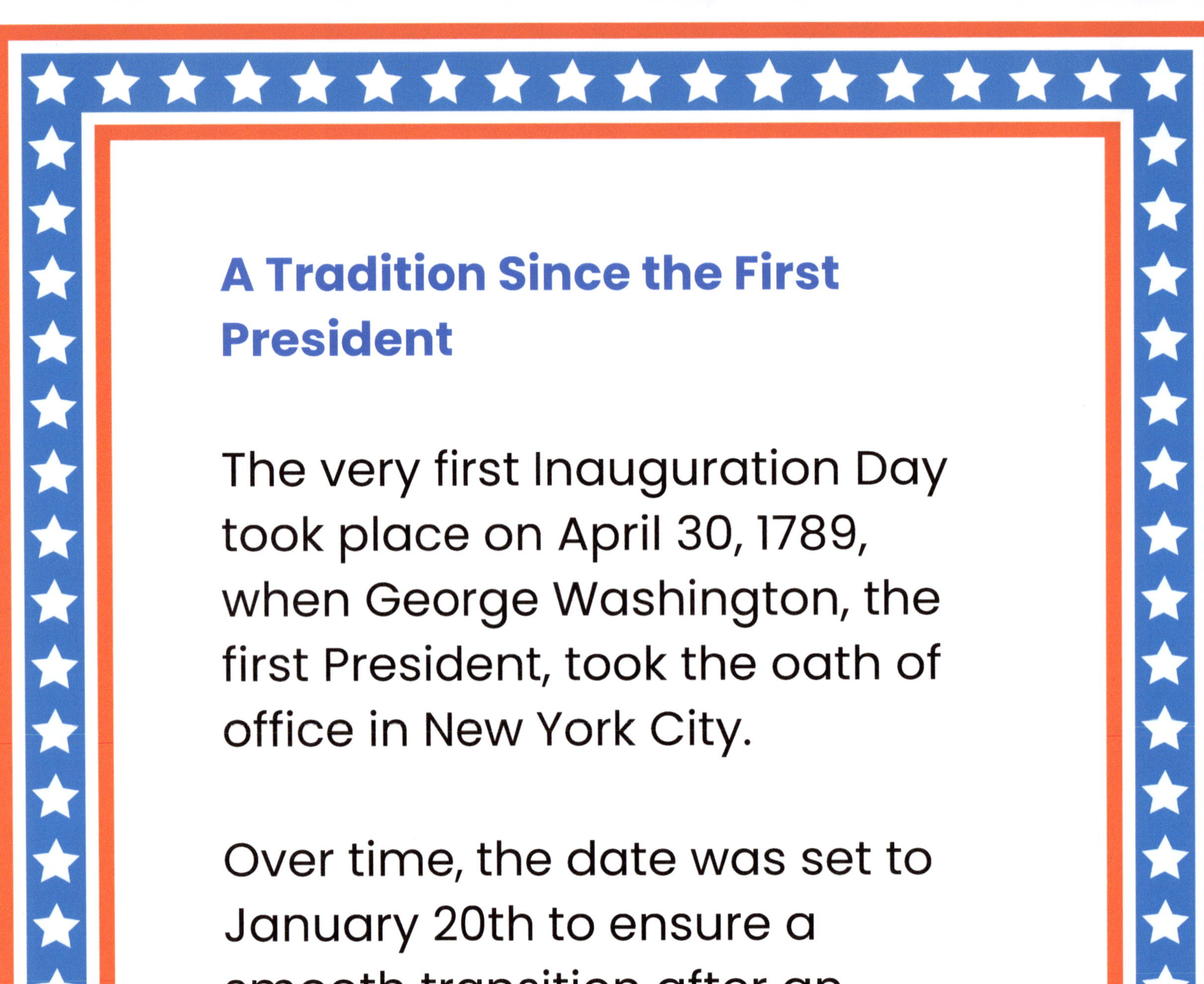

A Tradition Since the First President

The very first Inauguration Day took place on April 30, 1789, when George Washington, the first President, took the oath of office in New York City.

Over time, the date was set to January 20th to ensure a smooth transition after an election.

What Happens on This Day?

The highlight of Inauguration Day is when the President-elect recites the Oath of Office, promising to faithfully carry out their duties.

This oath is found in the U.S. Constitution and must be said before the new President begins their job.

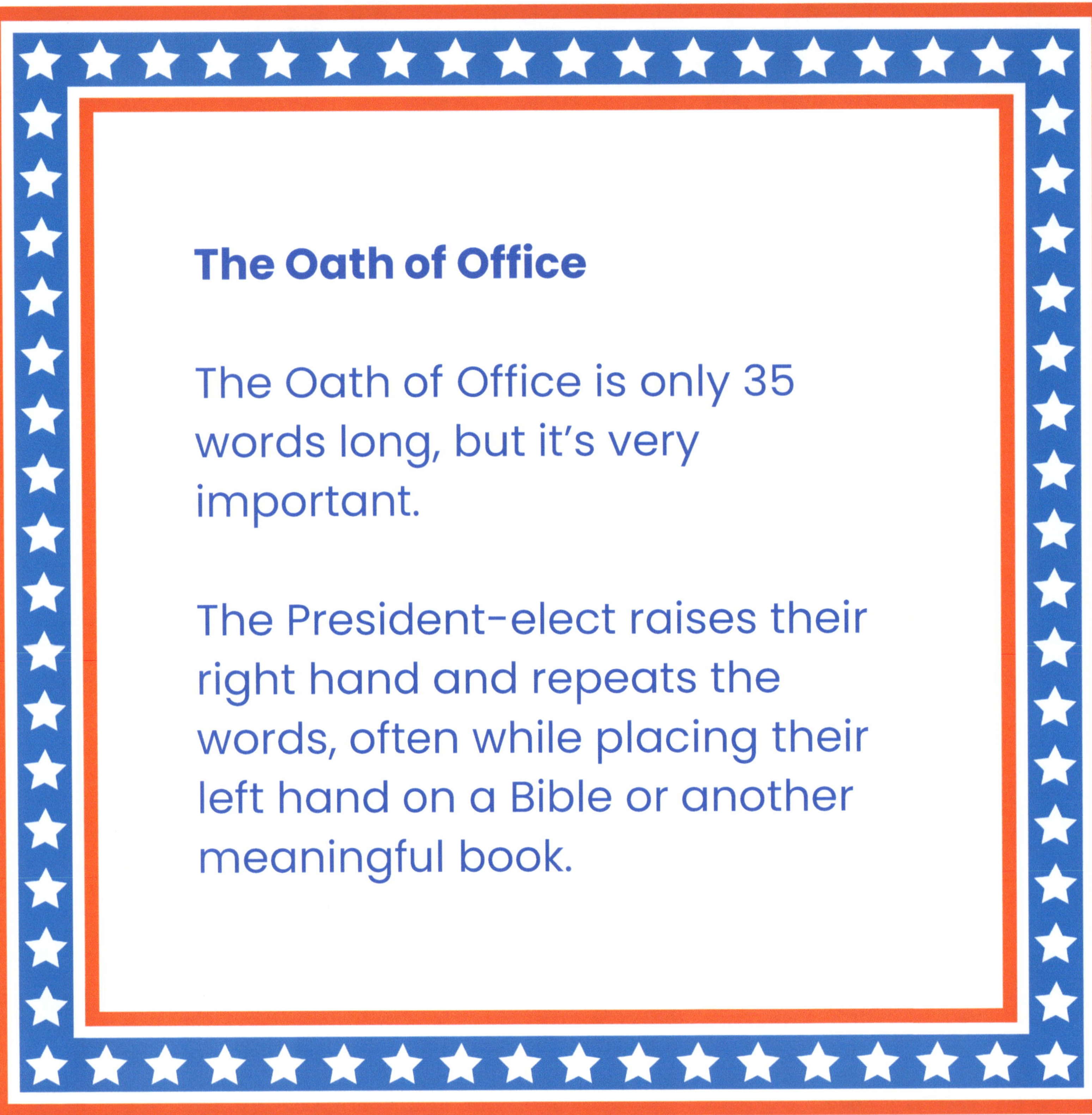

The Oath of Office

The Oath of Office is only 35 words long, but it's very important.

The President-elect raises their right hand and repeats the words, often while placing their left hand on a Bible or another meaningful book.

A Peaceful Celebration

Inauguration Day is more than just a ceremony; it's a celebration of democracy.

It shows the peaceful transition of leadership, even after heated elections.

This tradition is what makes the United States unique in the world.

Parades and Festivities

After the oath is taken, there's usually a grand parade in Washington, D.C., featuring marching bands, floats, and people celebrating.

The new President and Vice President often wave to crowds while riding down Pennsylvania Avenue.

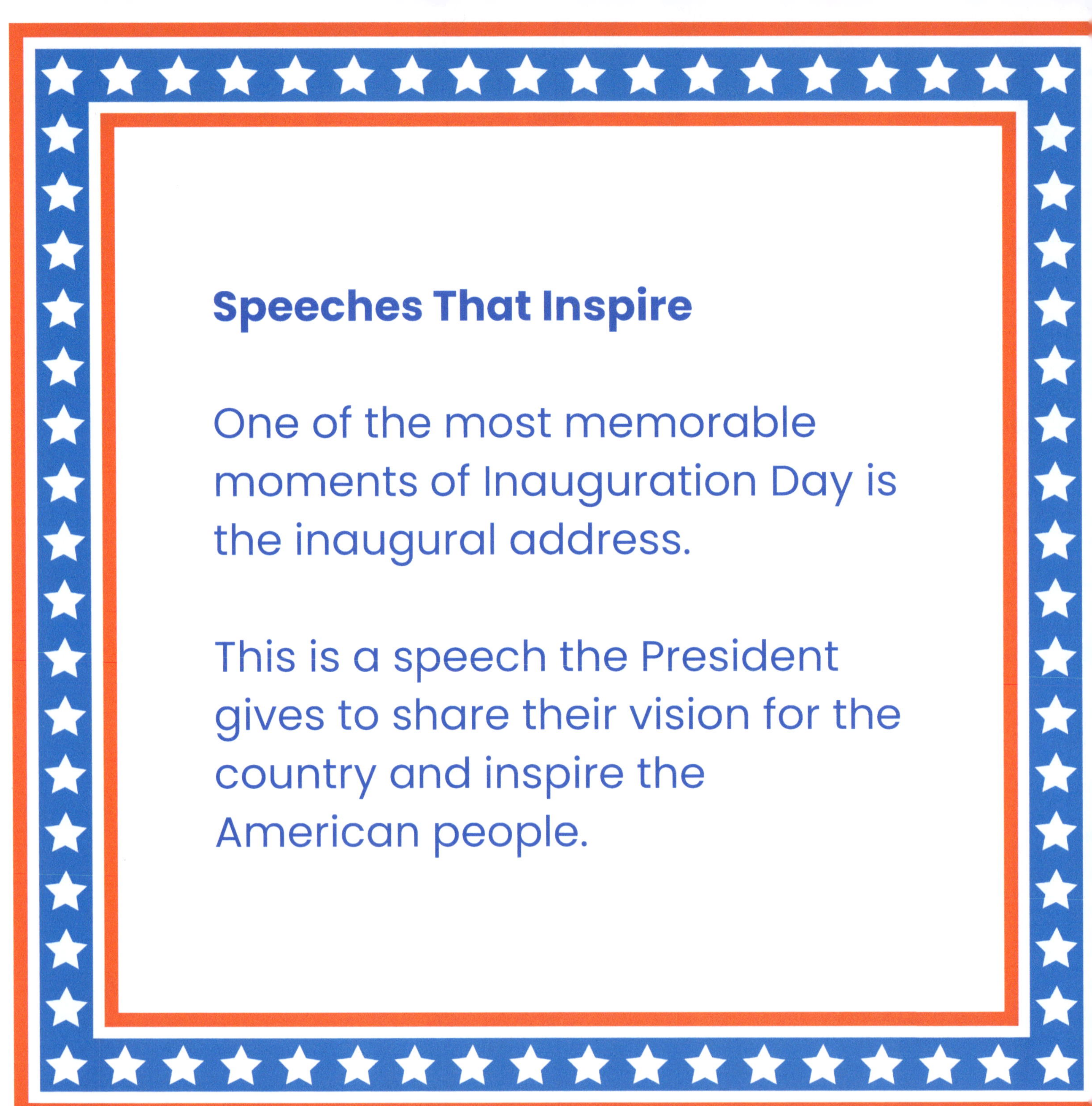

Speeches That Inspire

One of the most memorable moments of Inauguration Day is the inaugural address.

This is a speech the President gives to share their vision for the country and inspire the American people.

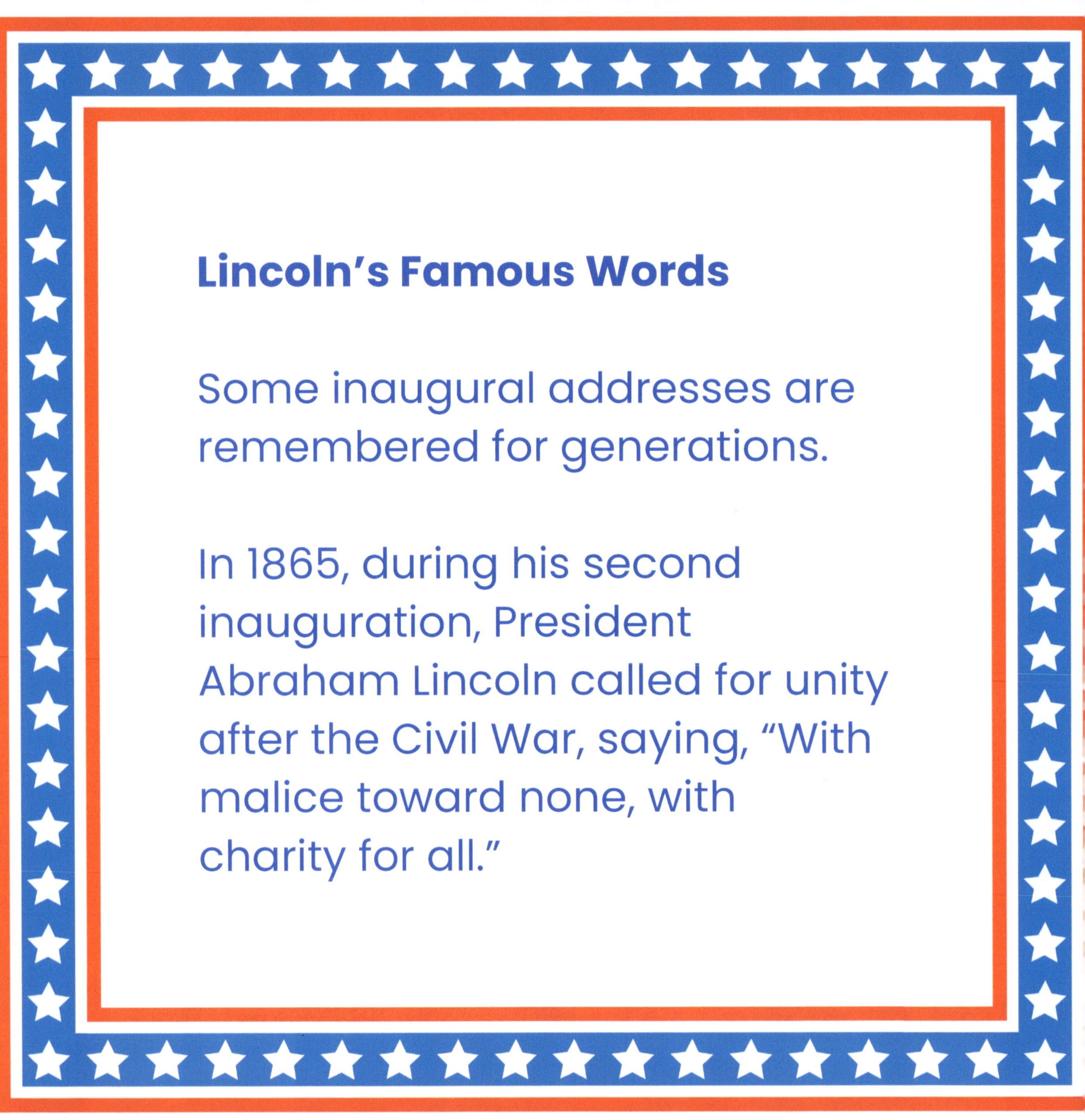

Lincoln's Famous Words

Some inaugural addresses are remembered for generations.

In 1865, during his second inauguration, President Abraham Lincoln called for unity after the Civil War, saying, "With malice toward none, with charity for all."

The First Lady's Role

The First Lady also plays an important part on Inauguration Day.

She may host events, wear a special outfit, and represent the United States with grace and elegance.

Children at the Ceremony

Did you know kids are often part of Inauguration Day?

Past Presidents have included their children and grandchildren in the ceremony, making it a family event.

Inauguration Balls

In the evening, Inauguration Day continues with fancy parties called inaugural balls.

These events are filled with music, dancing, and celebrations of the new leadership.

A Day for Everyone

Inauguration Day isn't just for politicians.

People from all over the country, and even the world, watch on TV or in person to feel part of this important moment in history.

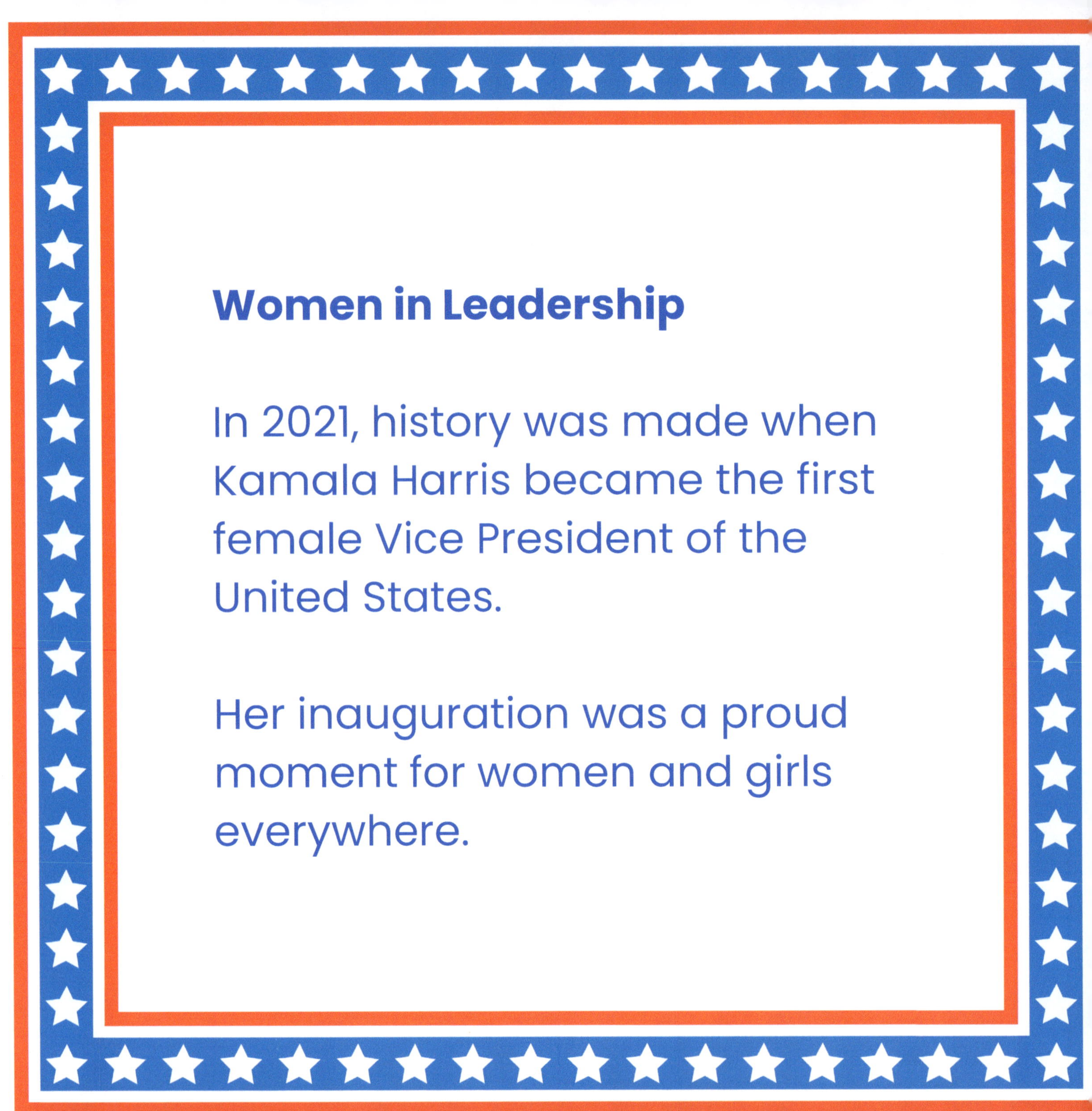

Women in Leadership

In 2021, history was made when Kamala Harris became the first female Vice President of the United States.

Her inauguration was a proud moment for women and girls everywhere.

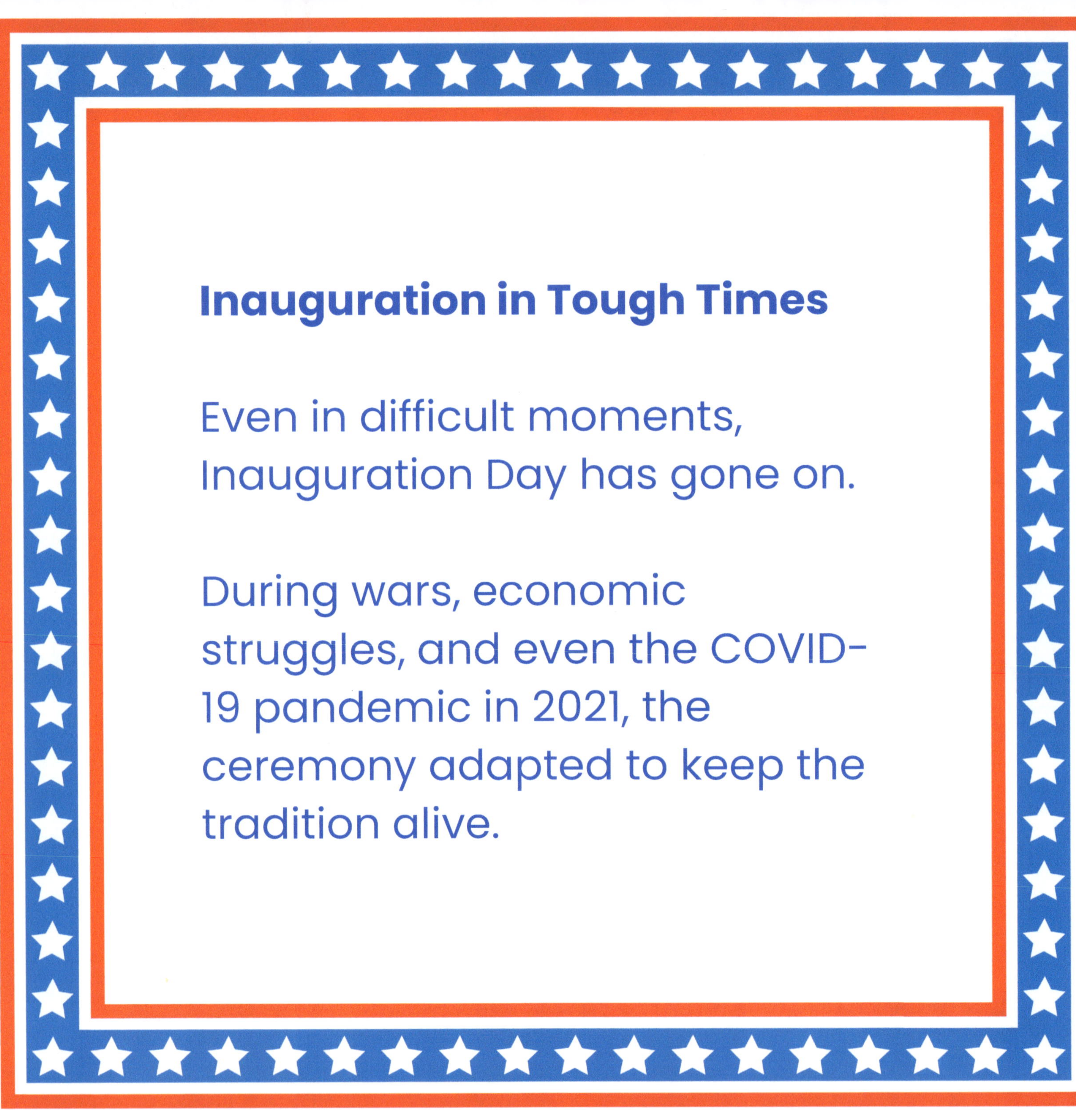

Inauguration in Tough Times

Even in difficult moments, Inauguration Day has gone on.

During wars, economic struggles, and even the COVID-19 pandemic in 2021, the ceremony adapted to keep the tradition alive.

A Tradition of Hope

Every Inauguration Day is a reminder of hope and a fresh start.

It's a day to reflect on the past and look forward to the future of the nation.

What Does It Mean to You?

Inauguration Day belongs to every American, no matter their age.

It reminds us that democracy works best when everyone's voice is heard.

What would you say if you were giving your own inaugural speech?